**How to Grow Potatoes: Planting and Harvesting Organic Food
From Your Patio, Rooftop, Balcony, or Backyard Garden**

How to Grow Potatoes: Planting and Harvesting Organic Food From Your Patio, Rooftop, Balcony, or Backyard Garden

By R.J. Ruppenthal, Attorney/Professor/Garden Writer

Contents

Chapter 1: Why Grow Potatoes? Five Great Reasons

Potatoes are one of the simplest food crops to grow at home. In this booklet, you will learn how to plant and grow potatoes in any sized garden. Even if you have no garden at all, and merely a doorstep, patio, rooftop, balcony, or deck, you can grow potatoes in very small spaces. Learn which type of containers potatoes thrive in, producing bigger harvests than you'll ever get from a bed in the ground. Learn how to select potatoes that mature earlier than others, giving you a quick harvest even in a short season climate with cold winters.

Be More Self-Sufficient

No other food crop allows you to do so much with so little as the potato. In fact, this is the most productive food staple you can produce at home. Just imagine how much space it would take to grow enough wheat, rye, oats, barley, or rice to feed a family. Yet you can grow enough potatoes on your doorstep to feed a person for days.

Potatoes pack more food energy per square foot than anything else you can grow. The only other food that even comes close is corn, but corn cannot touch the humble spud. Potatoes can produce more than 15,000 pounds per acre, while corn produces closer to 6,000 pounds. Here are the yields of some common food staples in terms of calories per acre. Yes, I know you and I are dealing in square feet (and maybe even square inches), but this gives you a sense of potato power:

Potatoes: 17.8 million calories per acre

Corn: 12.3 million calories per acre

Wheat: 6.4 million calories per acre

Soybeans: 2.1 million calories per acre

Beef: 1.1 million calories per acre

No wonder the Irish, with a difficult growing climate and poor soil, mono-cropped with potatoes. Prior to the potato famine of 1845-49, the average person in Ireland was eating about seven pounds of potatoes per day (and not much else). Currently, the average American eats 140 pounds of potatoes per year, or about 1/3 pound per day. For perspective, that is equal to one medium-sized Idaho russet potato every day.

It is important to eat a broad diversity of foods. I will never encourage you to eat only potatoes or to make potatoes the main part of your diet. But because we will discuss potato yields in this book, I want you to keep those consumption figures in mind. It will help keep things in perspective.

For example, if you learn in a later chapter that you can grow 15 pounds of potatoes in a certain type of container, you will know that this yield could allow you to eat one potato a day (the American consumption average) for at least 40 days. And in case of an emergency (hurricane, earthquake, prolonged power outage, etc.), keeping a few of these containers in service and near harvest would ensure several days' worth of emergency rations for a family of four.

Let's hope you never need this security, but it never hurts to be prepared. If you doubt the importance of good emergency preparation, then please watch some video clips of natural disasters and their aftermath. The aftermath of Hurricane Katrina in 2005 was enough to scare me. We cannot rely on the government to provide for us every time.

Potatoes are Nutritious

Potatoes provide much of the nutrition your body needs on a daily basis. One medium-sized potato delivers 110 fat-free calories, 45% of your daily need for vitamin C, 18% of your needed potassium, 10% of your vitamin B6, 8% each of your vitamin B1 and B3, 6% each of your iron, folate, phosphorus, and magnesium, plus plenty of other minerals in smaller concentrations.

Much of the nutrition is located in the potato skin, so you need to leave this on when you eat. Of course this is easier to eat the skin with tender new potatoes than leathery russet potatoes. Unfortunately, there is one more reason you might not want to east the skin: it may be full of pesticides.

Conventionally-grown (Non-organic) Potatoes are Covered with Pesticides

The United States government regularly tests for pesticide residue on food through the USDA Pesticide Data Program. Each year, an organization called the Environmental Working Group

(EWG) comes up with its "Dirty Dozen" and "Clean Fifteen" lists of fruit and vegetables by analyzing this pesticide data from the United States government. Potatoes made the "Dirty Dozen" list once again this year, showing higher pesticide residue levels than any other fruit or vegetable.[1]

In the most recent year, testing revealed that 37 pesticides are used on conventional potatoes. These include known carcinogens, neurotoxins, hormone disruptors, and reproductive toxicants. The EWG analysis showed that 84% of potato samples tested contained at least one bug killer or weed killer. No wonder we use so much ketchup on our fries.

Here, I will repeat two paragraphs from my *Blueberries in Your Backyard* book, since I cannot re-state the dangers of pesticides any more effectively than these experts can. If you are interested in that short book, you can find it on Amazon.

You do not want to consume these pesticides and you certainly do not want to feed them to your kids. According to natural health and wellness expert Dr. Andrew Weil, pesticides are "associated with a host of very serious health problems in people, including neurological deficits, ADHD, endocrine system disruption and cancer. Whenever possible, avoid exposure to pesticides, including pesticide residues on food."[2]

Dr. Harvey Karp, pediatrician and author of The Happiest Baby on the Block *added: "I really worry that pesticides on food are unhealthy for the tender, developing brains and bodies of young children... Studies show even small amounts of these chemicals add up and can impair a child's health when they're exposed during the early, critical stages of their development. When pesticide sprayers have to bundle up in astronaut-like suits for protection, it's clear parents want to feed their families food containing as little of these toxic chemicals as possible."[3]*

In Washington state, the nation's second-largest producer of potatoes after Idaho, growers applied more than 19 million pounds of pesticides on their potato crop in a recent year. However, a study from Washington State University determined that organic farming practices actually create larger and more productive potato plants.[4]

Some commercial potato farmers will not eat the potatoes they grow, since these are so heavily sprayed. These growers are known to keep their own "homegrown" potato patches, away from the main crop, which are clear of any sprays. Sadly, only 1% of Washington's potatoes are grown organically.

When you grow your own potatoes at home, you will not have to play Russian roulette with your health. You can eat potatoes and feed them to your kids, knowing they are grown in good soil that makes them nutritious. Just as importantly, you'll know what your potatoes don't contain. Grow as many as you can at home, and the rest of the time, try to buy organic.

---

[1] http://www.ewg.org/foodnews/summary
[2] http://www.ewg.org/foodnews/press
[3] Id.
[4] http://seattletimes.nwsource.com/html/localnews/2012250093_taters01m.html

Great for Kids

Kids love picking potatoes. Finding those white, gold, purple, and red tubers in the soil is like uncovering buried treasure. If you cannot get your kids to eat their vegetables, try involving them in the garden (even if it's just one container on your doorstep). When kids see where their food comes from and share in the excitement of harvesting it, everything changes. They become far more likely to eat and enjoy their veggies (okay, not all their veggies, but more than before).

Many vegetables in our garden (cucumbers, carrots, snap peas, and tomatoes) never even make it into the kitchen. Kids eat them on the spot. This does not hold true with spuds, which are cooked before eating, but they're quite the popular item after that. One of our kids loves potatoes and the other one doesn't, but both are eager to eat them once reminded that "these are the potatoes you picked." It makes a huge difference.

Do not rely on my opinion alone. Read an article entitled, "Children Eat More Fruits and Vegetables If They Are Homegrown", in Science Daily. The article reported on a study at Saint Louis University. The study provided clear evidence that kids who eat homegrown produce are twice as likely to eat their fruits and veggies every day. This is, most likely, a lifetime benefit.[5]

Save Yourself Some Money

Some foods we buy are very expensive in the stores, yet easy to grow at home. This is true with blueberries, the subject of another short book I wrote. Blueberries cost up to $11/pound in supermarkets. Yet the bushes thrive like weeds in the home garden, producing plenty of berries once you put them in the right soil.

In contrast, taters are pretty cheap to buy. If you're like the average American, eating 140 pounds of taters per year, your spud addiction may only cost you $50-100 per year. But it costs you more if you buy a lot of highly processed potato foods, such as chips, fries, or ready-made mashed potatoes. You can save much of this cost by growing some of your own spuds.

But if this doesn't look like much, there's another way in which you can save more. Here's how: The average person needs to consume 2000 calories per day (give or take a few). Potatoes are capable of supplying that kind of energy to your body.

How are you getting those calories now? What foods are you eating to supply you with energy? How much are you paying for them? Could you replace some of this cost with potatoes that are much cheaper (and perhaps more nutritious) than what you're eating now?

Food prices can go up and down (usually up), and they vary in different regions, but here is a ballpark estimate for some commonly-consumed, grain-based food staples. Prices were calculated through personal research or using numbers supplied by the government's Bureau of Labor Statistics.[6] All are whole grain products, and I used price per pound numbers so these can be compared easily with potatoes.

---

[5] http://www.sciencedaily.com/releases/2007/04/070418163652.htm
[6] http://www.bls.gov/ro3/apmw.htm

Bread (whole wheat): $2.02/pound

Spaghetti and macaroni noodles: $1.31

Brown rice: $1.59

Corn, frozen: $2.50

Potatoes: $0.69 (your own potatoes: almost $0)

Cheerios breakfast cereal: $4.00

I don't know what you like to eat, but if you were to eat a homegrown baked potato once per week instead of a side of corn or two pieces of toast, you might well save some money. Of course, you will save much more if you replace one highly-processed meal with homegrown, home-cooked potatoes. Remember, cooking a potato is easy as putting it in the microwave for a few minutes, while making roasted potatoes, fries, or a casserole takes longer. Baked potatoes themselves are pretty bland, but add some chopped green onions, chives, shredded cheese, sour cream, yogurt and/or bacon bits, and you have a meal (I understand this costs more than just the potato, but not much more per meal). Here are some examples of what you might replace, and what costs you might save:

Lasagna meal (microwave): $2.00-$4.00 (replace one per week: save $100-$200/year)
Mac-and-cheese (microwave): $1.66-$3.50 (replace one per week: save $86-$182/year)
Steamed brown rice bowl: $1.69 (replace one per week: save $88/year)
Corn soufflé (microwave): $3.92 (replace one per week: $200/year)

So at the end of the day, saving money with potatoes is about making small lifestyle changes. As long as you are cooking your own food, even with a grain-based diet, your food costs should be pretty low already. The only way to save big money is to replace a processed meal with one based on homegrown food, which requires slightly more prep time. If you are willing to do this, even once or twice a week, you will save a lot of money. Having homegrown potatoes on hand makes the task pretty simple.

Potatoes and eggs are a natural combination for nutrition, providing you with balanced protein and nearly all of the nutrients your body needs. They taste great for breakfast and other meals: omelet and hash browns, fried eggs over mashed potatoes, poached eggs and roasted spuds. If you like growing potatoes, consider getting a couple of chickens for your backyard also. They can eat a lot of your kitchen scraps and provide you with manure which can be tossed in a composter and then used to grow your next round of potatoes! For a simple beginner's guide to raising chickens, please see my *Backyard Chickens for Beginners* book, also available on Amazon.

Chapter 2: Different Kinds of Potatoes

If you have only eaten store-bought potatoes in the past, then chances are you have only eaten a few different varieties of potatoes. There are many more you can grow at home, so get ready for some tasty treats! Here is an overview of some different categories of potatoes, explained by function. Examples of potato varieties are provided in each group.

Below these descriptions, I have also included more information on where to buy certified disease free seed potatoes. Many local nurseries order seed potatoes of the most popular varieties around planting time in early spring. Alternatively, you can use your own potatoes for seed (purchased at a grocery store or grown yourself the year before). However, there is a risk of contamination with soil diseases. You can avoid this issue by buying certified disease free potatoes, either every year or every few years. They are not too expensive.

Reds, golds, purples, and fingerlings

Fingerlings: These are elongated little potatoes which resemble fat fingers. Even though they are small, these are mature potatoes grown from special fingerling varieties. Their taste is very tender and they are often used by gourmet chefs. Fingerlings come in different colors, including yellow, pink, and purple. Common varieties include: Rose Finn, La Ratte, Russian Banana, Austrian Crescent, Swedish Peanut, Red Thumb, French Fingerling, and Purple Peruvian.

Baking (Floury) Potatoes: Starchy varieties of potato are perfect for mashing, baking, and making into French fries. Favorite bakers include: any of the Russet types, Idaho, Cal White, Goldrush, Red Pontiac, Norkotah, All Blue, Mozart, and Snow White.

Boiling Potatoes: Waxy varieties of potato have more moisture and sugar than the baking types. They can be boiled, roasted, or barbecued. They will hold their shape well in soup, casserole, and potato salad. Good choices here include: Red Norland, Caribe, Yellow Finn, Charlotte, Maris Piper, and any of the Fingerlings mentioned above.

All Purpose Potatoes: These varieties can be boiled, mashed, fried, or baked. Some of the best-tasting potatoes are in this category: Kennebec, Yukon Gold, Purple Viking, Klondike Rose, Bintje, Salem, and German Butterball.

Best-Tasting Potatoes: This is a matter of personal preference, but some varieties are clear winners. Bintje is the world's most widely grown potato, a white variety that makes flavorful fries. La Ratte Fingerlings have been a longtime favorite of gourmet chefs. For those who love the robust flavor of red-skinned potatoes, Red Norland is hard to beat, but it is not the only red potato with great flavor. Yukon Gold, a very tasty potato that has been widely available in supermarkets, has justifiably gained a large following for its soft creaminess. For home gardeners, German Butterball often comes out on top. Some growers who have tasted their own homegrown German Butterball spuds have vowed they will never again grow or eat another potato. There are a growing number of other Butterball varieties available also.

New Potatoes (Baby Potatoes): New potatoes are small spuds that are picked before maturity. They usually measure only two or three inches in diameter. They have a fresh, tender taste, and can be cooked and eaten whole, since their skins have not had a chance to harden. New potatoes are best harvested around the time that your potato plants begin to flower, or just after the green foliage has peaked, before it begins to wither and turn brown. If you see the leaves begin to wither, you can either pick all your little potatoes at that time or you can reach down and steal a few new potatoes, letting the others continue to grow as the plant transfers its energy to the growing tubers.

Spuds picked early are deliciously tender

Purple ("Blue") Potatoes: Purple potatoes are a novelty and have become much more widely available in recent years. They make great visual presentations and are a nice addition to a "rainbow" potato dish. I have never found one that I like to eat as much as some of the lighter colored or red potatoes, but purple potatoes are very healthy for you. Research has shown that purple-fleshed potatoes have twice as many antioxidants as light-colored potatoes. Adirondack Blue, All Blue, Purple Majesty, and Purple Peruvian are some good examples. Don't be fooled by Viking Purple, which is purple on the outside but bright white inside.

Rainbow Mix: Try growing a mix of different colors. Pick anything from the purple category above, all of which are stunningly dark. For some red/pink flair, try All Red or Mountain Rose (which have pink skin AND mostly pink flesh) or French Fingerling, which has pink skin plus streaks in its white flesh. Then pick any yellow-fleshed potato, such as Charlotte, Carola, or Desiree (pink skin, yellow flesh). And throw in a white spud like Early Ohio, Sunrise, or Anoka. The brightest white flesh often can be found on potatoes with colored skins, such as Cherry Red, Red Dale, or Viking. And of course, you could sneak in an orange-fleshed sweet potato…

Early, Mid-Season, and Late Potatoes

Early potatoes are varieties that mature in shorter periods of time, generally around 60-80 days. They can be grown in short season climates, but do not keep well because they often have tender skins and high moisture content. Examples include: Caribe, Red Dale, Red Norland, Yukon Gold, Russet Norkotah, and Cal White (which holds the record for heaviest commercial yields).

Mid-season varieties take 80-100 days to mature. Members of this category share some of the characteristics of both early and late season spuds. The first fingerling to mature, Russian Banana, fits in this category. Other examples include: Katahdin, Anoka, German Butterball, Purple Majesty, Kennebec, Desiree, and Red Pontiac (the best red potato for long term storage).

Late potatoes are those that need a long growing season (100 days or more) to mature, such as Bintje, Yellow Finn, Rio Grande Russet, and All Blue. They tend to be better keepers and thus can be kept in storage for many months.

Where to Buy Seed Potatoes

Local nurseries usually have some seed potatoes available in early spring. These are the small, sprouting potatoes we use to grow spud plants. If you want more variety, buy your seed potatoes online. Order in the wintertime for the best selection; potatoes are normally shipped in March or April. Even if they arrive early, they will keep just fine in a cool location until you are ready to plant in the springtime. Here are some highly reputable sources of certified disease-free potatoes. Some of these offer organic choices as well.

1. Irish Eyes Garden Seeds: http://irisheyesgardenseeds.com

2. Potato Garden (formerly Ronniger Potato Farm and Milk Ranch Specialty Potatoes, which combined forces): www.potatogarden.com

3. Maine Potato Lady: www.mainepotatolady.com

4. Fedco Seeds' Moose Tubers: www.fedcoseeds.com/moose.htm

5. Territorial Seed Company: www.territorialseed.com

Chapter 3: Growing Potatoes in Containers, Raised Beds, and Traditional Rows

Potatoes can grow in anything that holds soil or mulch. An old bathtub, an old tire, or an old suitcase are examples of re-purposed items that gardeners have filled with soil to grow potatoes. You can grow potatoes in the ground in garden rows, as generations before us have done. You can grow them in raised beds, which tend to improve the productivity of every garden plant, potatoes included. Or you can grow them in any sort of container that holds enough soil volume.

Let's start by discussing containers. I have written several books and articles on growing vegetables, fruits, and berries in the home garden. For all of these crops, I strongly recommend putting them in raised beds if at all possible. Raised beds are my #1 choice because their deep, loose soil is a real benefit to the plants. I have never written anything where I recommended ground beds or containers over raised beds. Until now.

With potatoes, I am breaking with tradition to recommend containers as the best growing option. This recommendation is not only for people with apartments and no yard space; containers are best for potatoes anywhere. Believe it or not, containers just grow more potatoes. You will not get as many taters from either garden beds or raised beds as you will get from containers.

This is wonderful news for small space gardeners, because containers may be your only option. For everyone else, even if you have acres of land to farm, you may want to consider growing spuds in containers. Potatoes grown in containers will give you a bigger reward for your time and trouble, and they're the easiest spuds to harvest. That said, we will cover all three growing options here: containers, garden beds, raised beds. Let's start with containers.

Growing Potatoes in Containers

I have no green thumb when it comes to potatoes. I often put them in containers on the patio and then forget to water them for periods of time. And these potato containers sit on a windswept patio, taking a direct hit from strong coastal gusts that have outmatched many other plants. Yet I routinely harvest 10-14 pounds of potatoes from each of the 10-gallon containers they grow in.

Each of these containers holds less than two cubic feet of soil. If you took this same amount of soil and spread it on the ground, you would be very lucky to harvest 5-7 pounds of potatoes from it (which would be an amazing yield). How is it that I regularly harvest twice that quantity of spuds from similarly sized containers?

The secret is to use the right kind of container: a fabric pot or plastic grow bag works best. These containers have started popping up all over the place at nurseries, some of them with names like "potato grow bag" or "tomato grow bag". Their growing popularity is well deserved.

Fabric pots are made from a long-lasting cloth that is sown in the shape of a round cylinder. Most growing bags are made from woven plastic in the shape of either a round cylinder or deep shopping bag. A few of them include handles for hanging or carrying, while others feature a Velcro-secured side panel that opens for simple potato harvesting. If you have some extra burlap sacks, these could be filled with soil and used with a similar effect.

The most important feature of these pots/bags is that the cloth is porous. There are lots of tiny holes on the sides and bottom to let in air. When the roots of most plants encounter air, they stop, turn, and try another direction. This is known as root pruning or air pruning. Potato plants' roots branch out when they hit the air, extending the root system downward and creating more space for tuber growth. With potatoes, having more roots means harvesting more potatoes underground.

These pots/bags are usually dark in color, black or green, which allows the soil to warm up more quickly each day. This speeds plants' growth, even in cool spring and fall weather. But unlike some other kinds of pots, fabric pots and plastic growing bags do not overheat easily. Those same porous holes that prune the roots also keep the soil aerated. Good soil aeration is hugely important for the roots of many plants, especially potatoes, which produce better in loose soil than compacted soil.

It all adds up to a winning combination for these fabric pots and plastic grow bags. They provide the ideal environment for growing potatoes, and bags can be reused time and time again. If you cannot find either of these at a local nursery, order some online. Here are some good suppliers.

Smart Pots: The 10 and 15 gallon sizes are perfect for patios, balconies, rooftops, and decks. There are a variety of different kinds sold on Amazon. They also retail them on their own site here: http://www.smartpots.com.

Grow Bags from Gardeners Supply: This company always carries the trendiest new garden containers. They offer an extensive selection of grow bags for planting potatoes, tomatoes, salad greens, and herbs (all these crops can grow in them, but none of the others outperform the way that potatoes do). http://www.gardeners.com

Park Seed: Retails the plastic potato grow bags as well. http://parkseed.com

Alternatively, try running an online search for "potato grow bags" and you will see plenty of other buying options.

Growing Potatoes in Raised Beds and Garden Rows

Potatoes will grow just fine in either garden rows or raised beds, but the ones grown in raised beds will be more productive. That is because the soil is deep, loose, and probably of richer quality than what is under your garden. All these factors favor more potato production.

But if you have your heart set on raising spuds in traditional rows, then I won't stop you. There is something very fulfilling about growing plants in the native soil of your own yard. And you will be joining generations of people who have grown their own food the traditional way.

The practice of growing spuds in rows and raised beds is about the same. Since we will cover planting and care of potatoes in the next two chapters, I will focus this section on what you need to know about gardening in rows and in raised beds.

Garden Rows

There are two major benefits of row gardening as well as some downsides. First, there is no major cost associated with row gardening, such as there would be if you purchased containers or building materials for raised beds. If you have decent soil in your yard, you can just plant your potatoes and start growing. Your productivity will be better if you prepare the soil first, and this can cost a few dollars for some good soil amendments. But even with this, your overall startup cost will be either free or very cheap.

The second major benefit with row gardening is that your plants have access to the water and minerals that occur in your soil. Deep rooted plants can continue drawing moisture from ground soil for a long time, whereas containers and raised beds dry out much more quickly than most garden soils. And the plants are not reliant on you to provide 100% of their nutritional requirements, since they can draw some minerals from the ground.

If you are starting a garden in a part of the yard that has never been used to make beds before, then you will need to dig up the soil and prepare it. First, mow any grass or weed as low as you can. Mark off the area you wish to use and the proper size of beds. These can be any length that fits your space, and any width from 1-3.5 feet. With wider rows, you are preparing a larger growing area for plants, and therefore they should be happier and more productive. Yet they should not be too wide that you cannot reach the very middle of the bed to plant, fertilize, weed, tend, or harvest there. Mark the intended beds with chalk, string laid on the ground, or stakes in the four corners.

Crowding plants does not improve their production. As discussed in the next chapter, proper potato plant spacing is about 12 inches apart in the row. Leave at least 30 inches between separate rows when measured from the row centers where the plants will grow.

Once you have your space marked off, use a shovel or spade to dig up a chunk of soil that is 6-12 inches deep. If the top is covered with grass or weeds, try your best to scalp it and turn the weed side down. Then use the shovel or spade to break up the soil as well as possible. If your soil is light and easy to work, then you are fortunate. If it has a lot of sand or clay in it, then you will need to amend it by working in plenty of organic matter, such as compost, manure, leaves, peat, or grass clippings. If it has lots of rocks or is pure clay, then you may want to consider investing in some containers or building your garden upwards (with a raised bed) rather than downwards. Repeat this process chunk by chunk, square foot by square foot, until you have dug up and loosened the soil in the whole bed area.

Most soil is usable and can be improved with organic matter. After digging up the soil and breaking it up, cover it with an inch or two of good compost, manure, or other organic matter. Gently dig this in to the top of the upturned soil. Water the soil well after you dig it, since it can dry out very quickly. Potatoes can be planted immediately in these new beds. Don't forget to fertilize and water regularly (which we will discuss shortly). Your potatoes will grow fine the first year, but probably better the second year after that, once the soil has had a chance to stabilize and incorporate the organic matter you have added.

Digging beds is hard work. I can make it even harder for you if you would like to create more productive rows with deeper soil. When you dig up the soil, rather than replacing the scoopfuls of soil in the same place, remove them to a wheelbarrow or place them on the ground to the side of the row area. Once the soil has been scooped out for 6-12 inches deep, dig up a second, lower layer to the same depth and put that soil to the side again. Throw a little compost, manure, or organic matter in the bottom of the trench if you want. Then place the first (top level) scoops of soil weed side down and break them up with the shovel. This layer will become your subsoil. Repeat with the deeper soil, which now goes on top and gets mixed with compost or organic matter to become your new topsoil. Your beds now have been improved to an impressive growing depth. Your plants will be happy.

If you are on a strict timetable and need to plant right away, you can dig hills rather than rows. (Hills are not to be confused with the process of "hilling" by mounding soil around plants, which will be described soon in another chapter.) Hills are just holes you dig up to loosen and improve the soil in a small space, say 1-2 square feet. Dig one per potato plant, following the plant spacing suggestions above.

Just think of a row as a solid line and a set of hills as a dotted line. You can dig a lot of these, amend them with compost, and plant them with potatoes pretty quickly. Once the plants are in the ground, you'll have plenty of time to connect these dots into rows, if that is your intention, by digging up and improving the soil in between them.

Raised Beds

With raised beds, you can prepare the soil beneath them as described above if you want maximum growing depth. But most of the work involves building the raised bed upwards. A raised bed is any mounded bed of improved soil that is maintained higher than the ground level. However, for purposes of my explanation, a raised bed also needs walls. This allows you to create deeper, uncompacted soil without the whole mess falling over.

Constructing raised beds is well worth the trouble and added expense. They will pay for themselves soon enough with improved yields of any garden crop you grow there. The startup cost depends upon the materials used and what you pay for them. You can build raised bed walls out of wood, stone, bricks, cinderblocks, tires, plastic, metal, or any support material you can find. You may decide to avoid using old tires or treated wood because of the possibility of toxins leeching into the soil, but from the research I've seen on both of these, the quantities of leeched toxins should be very minimal. Raised beds can be built to any size that fits your space.

I have three raised beds and my backyard and four more in my front yard. Despite being a gardening writer, I am not much of a handyman when it comes to building things. But I purchased some rot resistant wood at my local big box store (redwood is cheapest in my region), cut them to size with a handsaw, and screwed them together into beds.

All my beds are rectangular, four feet by eight feet (4'x8'). First, I marked out the locations on the ground. Then I dug up the soil a bit. Next, I cut the wood to the right sizes, using four by four inch (4"x4") lumber for corner posts and flat two by eight inch (2"x8") or two by ten inch (2"x10") pieces for the walls. On later beds, I experimented by using thinner two by two inch (2"x2") corner posts, which seemed to work fine as well. I used 2-3 pieces of flat lumber on each side to make the beds 20-24 inches tall.

Here are two pictures of wooden raised beds. The first shows one of my backyard beds which is growing potatoes and broccoli on half as well as a permanent planting of blueberries on the side. As you can see, the second half has been left to the chickens, which debug the bed, fertilize the soil and aerate it with their scratching. After a few months, I move the temporary fence to another raised bed for them to scratch in, planting a short time later in the one they improved. The second picture below shows a shallower raised bed built from four pieces of lumber on a lawn.

Rot resistant wood (such as cedar or redwood) performs well over time, while other wood can be painted or stained with a non toxic coating. New lumber can be expensive, so you can save a good deal of money by using old, repurposed wood. When someone remodels a house or replaces a fence in your area, see if you can get some old wood. I prefer screws to nails, since they hold the wood more tightly. I even spent more for vinyl coated screws that would not rust.

Bricks, cinderblocks, or stones can be used to make either a temporary or permanent raised bed. Before I was sure I wanted a raised bed in a particular place, I stacked some bricks and cinderblocks that I had salvaged. They created a loose box that I filled with soil. If you do this, you need to be careful about bricks falling out, which they do frequently, but if you need a quick bed for one season, this will do the trick. For a more permanent bed, you can get some mortar and build strong walls with stones, bricks, or cinderblocks.

If you have a patio or walkway space that's covered in concrete or stone, you can build a bed on top of it. If the area is flat, a raised bed filled with soil should not move, so you do not need to affix it permanently into the ground. I built one on my patio and used wood siding plus four by four inch (4"x4") corner posts. The bed just sits on top of the patio surface like a big box. To protect the surface and prevent your soil from escaping, you can line the bottom with a few sheets of plastic and staple them to the insides of the walls or weigh them down with stones. Plastic sheeting is available at hardware stores.

The height matters. As you can see from the picture of the raised bed built on a lawn, the bed can be shallow and only raise the soil level by a few inches. It still helps, but potatoes are deep rooted enough that you still will need to vastly improve the subsoil beneath the bed. SO I would dig it up and prepare it as if I were growing in the ground soil directly, then build the bed on top and fill it with more soil or compost for growing.

On the other hand, a bed that is 12 inches or taller in height may not need access to the ground below. This is great for building on concrete, or if you have lousy soil filled with rocks or dominated by heavy clay. Just put in some plastic sheeting and/or a three inch layer of gravel at the bottom for a barrier. Other barriers at the bottom of the bed can include landscape fabric for weed suppression and poultry netting for preventing gophers, voles, and digging rodents from entering the bed. I cover the bottom of the bed, bring up the covering a few inches on each side, and staple it in with 14 mm staples.

There may be one more big expense involved in raised bed gardening. Once you build the bed, you have to fill it. You can use almost any combination of soil and compost as well as other ingredients like peat, sand, and low grade manure. The most cost effective mix that works well in raised beds is about 25% sand or perlite, 25-50% compost, and 25-50% peat moss. If you buy bag after bag of potting soil to fill larger beds, you will deplete your bank account, but this works fine for smaller beds. To fill a big void, it is more cost effective to order a delivery of planting mix or compost.

You can also start dumping in any other organic material you have in quantity, including herbicide free grass clippings, hedge trimmings, leaves, shredded paper, sawdust from untreated wood, layers of newspaper, coffee grounds, and kitchen waste. Bury this material under some soil or compost, keep it well watered, and it will all break down to give you some really good soil. You can plant in it right away and your potatoes will grow in it just fine, but the soil will be fabulous next year.

If potatoes are the only crop you plan to grow, you could even fill a raised bed or container with mulch (such as straw) instead of soil. Whatever you use to fill your raised beds, you should know that the soil level will drop by several inches in the coming months as organic materials decompose and the soil settles in. You may need to keep filling your beds with more soil or mulch for the first year or so. And it just so happens that potato plants are the most productive when you keep adding more soil or mulch around them. The next chapter describes this method more fully.

Chapter 4: Planting and Hilling Potatoes

Planting

Potato plants grow from chunks of old potatoes. Have you ever seen the "eyes" on an old potato start to sprout? That's what we put in the soil, and it grows up into a new plant. A large potato can be cut into several chunks, each one with an "eye" in it. With smaller potatoes, we just plant the whole potato.

Spuds beginning to sprout, perfect for seed potatoes

Potatoes grow best in the temperature range of 50-70 degrees (F). They have trouble in hot weather, so if you live in a hot summer climate, make sure to keep them well watered. You could even consider planting them in an area that gets some afternoon shade. Or you could cover them with a row cover or shade fabric. These are sold at nurseries in hot climate locations.

Since they like cool weather, potatoes make a great spring crop and often a successful fall crop as well. Early varieties of potatoes require around 60-80 days to reach maturity, so it is entirely possible that you may be able to grow two or more crops per season. At the very least, you may be able to get some tender new potatoes from a late crop. In a cool maritime climate that never gets too hot or too cold, you can grow potatoes year-round with little or no frost protection.

Traditionally, the first planting day is around St. Patrick's Day in mid March. This makes it easy to remember, but you need to remember to buy your seed potatoes before then. Potatoes planted in March should be ready by July. You could plant a second crop in a different location as late as June 15 and harvest them as late as possible, around the time of your first frost. If you live in a short season climate where the first frost can come as early as October 1st, then make sure to plant only early varieties of potatoes. And if you're not harvesting yet at that time, then make sure to cover your spuds with a nice, thick blanket of leaves or straw to protect them from the cold.

When you buy "seed potatoes" from a supplier, you are buying a bag of little potatoes. They are sold in one pound, two pound, five pound, or larger amounts. Some seed catalogs actually sell "potato seeds", which are a recent development, but these seeds produce a much less vigorous plant. The great thing about growing potatoes is that they store so much energy in those little tubers. Even a young plant that's run over with a lawnmower and loses all its leaves can grow back, because it can draw energy from the old potato under the soil until its leaves start converting energy from the sun. Even when you harvest potatoes, you often see that shriveled up old potato clinging to the vine underground; it still has a little energy and water in reserve.

Planting potatoes is pretty easy. Basically, we just bury the seed potato in the soil and it will grow, sending its stem shoot upwards and its roots downward. Space potato plantings about 12 inches apart from one another, and if you are planting in rows, then space rows at least 30 inches apart. You can plant the seed potato anywhere from 6-9 inches deep. In fact, you can plant it anywhere from 2-12 inches deep, but studies have shown that shallow potatoes suffer from frequent sunburn (and become toxic to eat), while deeper plantings result in less potato production.

Hilling

Though deeper planting is not better, many growers do achieve increased potato yields using a system called "hilling" or "trenching". You can do this in the ground, in a raised bed, or even in containers. The idea is to take advantage of potato plants' growing vigor and trick them into producing more spuds. Tater plants only form tubers in the root area above where they are planted in the ground. But if you bury their stems in soil as they grow, and continue to create a "hill" of soil where they grow, these stems will root and the plant will continue to grow upward. Hilling creates more root space for tuber production between the top of the soil and the level where the seed potato was planted. A traditional garden row, when hilled, looks like this:

But you don't need to build a hill above ground if you start at a lower level. First, dig a trench or series of holes 12 inches deep and plant the seed potatoes at the bottom. Cover these with 3-4 inches of soil or mulch. In a few days, the plants will start to emerge. When you see six inches of stem showing above ground, surround the bottom few inches of the stems with some more soil or mulch (such as straw, untreated sawdust, or leaves). Do not cover any of the leaves. Make sure you water in the new soil or mulch.

Then when the plants grow six more inches of stem above ground, repeat the process by placing more soil or mulch around them. Again, they will grow. Theoretically, you can continue doing this many more times (especially with late season varieties). But if you start the potatoes in a trench 12 inches deep, you will reach the surrounding soil level after two or three applications of soil/mulch. With hilling, the plants will produce many more potatoes in these top few inches of material.

Chapter 5: Soil, Fertilization, and Watering Potatoes

Good Soil or Mulch for Potatoes

Potatoes will grow in many kinds of soil. They will produce a few spuds even in poor soil. But to get productive yields of potatoes, they need good soil. Aim for a soil that is slightly on the acidic side, which is true of most garden soils. If you are growing your spuds in the ground, or if you have filled containers or raised beds with native soil, mix in some organic matter. Here, the term "organic" does not mean pesticide-free; it refers to material created by living plants or animals. Compost, aged manure, leaf litter, shredded paper, untreated sawdust, and lawn clippings are all great examples of organic matter that can be mixed into the soil to improve its health and structure.

Having plenty of organic matter in the soil ensures that it will retain more moisture, while also loosening the soil so that water and air flow to the plants' roots. Organic matter also decomposes slowly in the soil, nourishing an important community of beneficial organisms that provide nutrients for plants and improve their disease immunity. And it keeps the soil slightly acidic, which is what potatoes (and most plants) prefer.

You don't even need soil to grow spuds. Potatoes will grow fine in layered newspaper, straw, shredded paper, untreated sawdust, or fallen leaves (let's call these materials "mulch"). Plants need soil for physical support and nutrition. Potatoes can get the physical support they need from mulch, but they cannot derive much nutrition from it. So they'll only grow in mulch if you supply them with all the nutrients they need. I recommend sprinkling some balanced organic fertilizer into the soil and watering it in. Also, please see the last chapter ("Secret Tips"), which contains an additional fertilizing suggestion. You need to feed plants grown in soil, also, but they are capable of finding some soil minerals on their own.

Potato plant, above and below the soil

Feeding Your Plants

Feed potatoes by applying some balanced organic fertilizer to the soil. Here, the term "organic" refers to a product that is pesticide-free and does not contain chemically-synthesized ingredients. Organic fertilizers are made from whole foods which nourish the plants and improve the health of the soil. These can include ingredients like seed meal, aged poultry manure, feather meal, rock phosphate, bone meal, wood ash, or kelp meal.

Most nurseries and garden centers sell at least one brand of organic fertilizer. Large nationally-distributed brand names of organic fertilizers include Espoma, Dr. Earth, and Down To Earth, though you may find a good regional alternative as well. Any all-purpose garden or vegetable fertilizer (e.g. "Organic Vegetable Food") will do just fine, including any product that features tomatoes in its name or picture (e.g. "Tomato Garden Fertilizer"). Tomatoes are the most popular home gardening crop, and they are close relatives of potatoes, so their nutritional needs are similar.

All fertilizers have a set of three numbers printed on their bags, boxes, or labels. The numbers refer to the relative quantities of the three major plant nutrients: nitrogen (N), phosphate (phosphorus) (P), and potash (potassium) (K). A balanced fertilizer, such as one labeled with an N-P-K number of "5-5-5", is about right for potatoes, but do not worry if you cannot find one with those exact ratios. A "bulb and bloom" fertilizer with less nitrogen and higher levels of phosphate and potash (e.g. 3-6-6) also works well for potatoes grown in a soil that's rich in organic matter. Potatoes need some nitrogen, and if you hill them aggressively they will use more, but too much nitrogen will result in excess leaf growth at the expense of potato tubers.

Organic vegetable fertilizer (5-7-3)

Keeping Your Potatoes Watered

Keep your potatoes well watered. At least once a week (and more often in hot or dry weather), give them a deep soaking. They need about an inch of water per week, equivalent to perhaps 3-5 gallons per plant, though the actual amount will depend on your climate and soil. The water needs to penetrate down to the root system, not just moisten the top inch or two of soil. A deep watering is best accomplished with a slow drip irrigation system, soaker hose, or sprinkler (rather than by dumping a whole bucket of water on the plants all at once, which tends to create runoff).

You can minimize the need to water by mulching your potatoes. Straw, leaves, shredded paper, coconut coir, and cocoa bean hulls make great top mulches. Put a blanket of at least 3-4 inches of mulch on top of your soil to seal in the moisture and prevent evaporation; this can reduce your need to water by as much as 50-75%.

To determine if your plants need water, stick a finger into the soil. If the soil is dry an inch or two down, water it well. If you are growing your potatoes in organic matter mulch rather than soil (a method described in the previous chapter), then you will need to water more frequently at first, until the material absorbs some water. This material can dry out pretty quickly at first, but over time it will retain more moisture than typical soil.

Wet leaves are the culprit behind many leaf diseases. You can avoid this by watering in the morning, which will allow the leaves to dry out in the sun. Alternatively, watering with drip irrigation or a soaker hose delivers the water at the soil level, keeping the leaves mostly dry.

Increase watering by 50% when your potato plants begin to flower or when they have developed a large amount of green leafy foliage. This is the time when potato plants put their energy into growing the tubers. This growth stage requires more water if you want to harvest big potatoes.

At the end of the growing season, when the leaves wilt and start to turn brown, you can stop watering. The potatoes under the soil will develop tougher skins at this time, which will help increase their storage life. You also want the soil to be pretty dry when you harvest your spuds, because wet soil is harder to work with and it tends to stick to the potatoes.

Chapter 6: Harvesting

Now comes the fun part of digging for gold (or white, red, or purple). Once the potatoes are ready and the soil is fairly dry, simply dig them up. If you are growing in a container, another option is just to turn it over and dump out the soil, spreading this out on the ground so that potatoes are easy to see and pick out. When I do this on a patio, I generally use a covering such as some overlapped sheets of newspaper, which simplifies cleanup. When the kids harvest potatoes from containers, we use scoop-shaped trowels to dig out the soil, keeping two buckets nearby: one for the soil scoopings, and another to carry the potatoes.

To pick potatoes from a garden row or raised bed, you need a tool to dig the soil. Most people use shovels or spades for this. The best tool is a pitchfork (though not all urban gardeners have one). You can sink the fork into the soil beside the potato plants, push it towards and under the plants, and then pull any spuds upward. The fork tines offer very little resistance in the soil, allowing you to essentially filter it for potato tubers.

Harvesting potatoes with a shovel is clumsier, since the soil moves with it. To use a shovel effectively, you need to take slow, gentle scoops, being careful not to slice any potatoes in half. When using a shovel for this, I break up the bed into imaginary grid segments of one square foot apiece, digging up one at a time until the whole bed is completed. I slowly dump the soil out of the shovel on the side of the bed, picking out spuds as they appear.

If you have more time and patience, you can use a trowel and conduct a slower, archaeological excavation of the soil around the potatoes. This method probably ensures that you will not impale any spuds with your tool, but it seems to take forever in a large bed. The trowel is a better tool to use with containers, which have less soil volume.

As described in Chapter 2, new potatoes should be picked earlier, around the time that plants flower. You can either harvest all the spuds at this time, digging up the bed or emptying the container, or you can selectively "steal" a few spuds while allowing the plants and their remaining tubers to continue growing until maturity. To steal a few new potatoes, reach your hands into the soil under the plants and feel for some tubers. Gently pull them off the roots without pulling up the whole plant, which can be left to continue growing. New potatoes are tender and do not need to be peeled, but they won't keep very long: use them right away and enjoy!

Chapter 7: Storing Potatoes for Later Use

Late-maturing potatoes store the best. This also means you may be harvesting them as the weather turns cold. If frost comes before you can harvest, cover the potatoes with a blanket of mulch, such as leaves or straw, to protect them. Once you pick the potatoes, do not wash them. Unwashed potatoes store better.

The best place to store your potatoes will vary. A cool, dry root cellar is ideal. For most of us, a pantry, garage, or storage space with good air circulation is the best we can do. Ideal storage temperatures for potatoes are in the range of 45-55 F degrees, though anywhere from 40-60 degrees is acceptable for shorter periods. Do not put potatoes in the refrigerator unless you want them to become sweeter; the starches may convert to sugars in cold temperatures.

Before storing potatoes, inspect them and remove any tubers that have cuts or blemishes. These you can trim and eat immediately, if parts of them are still good. Store your spuds in paper bags, potato/onion mesh bags, or cardboard boxes. These materials breathe well, which is important, whereas potatoes stored in plastic bags become too humid and rot. A company called Orka makes these cloth bags that work well to store potatoes, onions, and root vegetables; they also save space since you can hang them from a hook.

Hanging storage bags for potatoes, onions, and root vegetables

Once upon a time, people could not get what they needed at a supermarket and had to store root vegetables to feed the family during winter. Those without root cellars often used a method called a storage clamp. Large clamps are still used in the agricultural industry to "warehouse" root crops outdoors until they are ready for market.

To make a clamp, you choose a dry part of the yard (or the side of a hill), dig a big hole, and line it with a thick layer of straw or shredded paper. Place one layer of potatoes or root vegetables on the straw, packed loosely to allow for air circulation. Cover this with another layer of the straw or shredded paper. You could use sand or sawdust just as easily. Place another layer of potatoes on top, cover it again, and repeat until you have filled most of the hole. Finally, cover it with a thick layer of straw on top, which you can hold in place with some scrap wood or stones. Take out a few potatoes as you need to use them, starting with the top layer and working downward.

A storage clamp works best if you have a large quantity of vegetables to store over the winter, particularly potatoes, onions, and root vegetables. This method also leaves your food vulnerable to soil-based pests such as gophers, voles, or digging rats. You might be able to strengthen your clamp by lining it first with sharp gravel and then straw, then covering the top with a tough piece of wood that is drilled with small air holes and heavily weighted down with stones or cinderblocks. Another option is to take an old refrigerator or barrel and bury it most of the way in the hole, layering and covering as you would with an open clamp. On a smaller scale, it probably makes more sense just to store a few pounds of potatoes in a cardboard box or paper bag in your home.

Wherever you put them, cover your potatoes well to block out any sunlight, which causes tubers to turn green and become toxic. As you select potatoes from storage to cook and eat, make a quick inspection to ensure there are no shriveled or rotten spuds in storage. If you find any, remove them.

Bonus Chapter: Two Secret Tips for Getting More (and More Delicious) Potatoes

If you put some seed potatoes in the ground and keep the plants watered as they grow, you *will* harvest some delicious homegrown potatoes. Potato plants are prolific enough that they do not need much care and are not too particular about soil. You will get a few pounds of potatoes, which probably will taste better than anything you have bought at the grocery store.

But if you treat them really well, you'll get many more potatoes, which will taste even better. What if you could double or triple your yield? And what if you could ensure that those spuds taste so good they are fit to be served at a gourmet restaurant? This final bonus chapter contains three suggestions for dramatically increasing your yield and ensuring that your plants grow the best tasting potatoes.

Secret Tip #1: Grow Potatoes Vertically for an Amazing Yield in a Very Small Space

Remember the chapter on hilling? Potatoes will keep growing upwards when you mound the soil around their stems. These stems root in the ground, creating more space for the formation of spuds underground. "Hilling" potatoes will dramatically increase your yield.

What if you grew potatoes in a very vertical environment, planting some late maturing potatoes at the beginning of the year, and just kept on hilling them again and again? How high would they grow and how many potatoes would they produce from a few square feet of growing space? The answers are 3-4 feet and 25-100 pounds.

Greg Lutovsky, owner of Irish Eyes Garden Seeds in Washington State, came up with plans for a box that can grow 100 pounds of potatoes in just four (4) square feet of horizontal growing space.[7] He personally grew 81 pounds of potatoes using this box (or "cage"), while a friend of his grew 124 pounds. These plans have been reported on in several media outlets, including the Denver Post[8] and Seattle Times.[9]

The basic idea is to build a frame for a vertical box two feet by two feet (2'x2') wide. The frame extends 3-4 feet high. You plant the potatoes in soil at the bottom and begin "hilling" by mounding the soil around the growing stems. As the soil and plant level rises, you also fill in the walls by nailing or screwing in a new board on the side each time. Eventually, the plants and box sides will reach the top. You can begin harvesting potatoes from the bottom by removing one of

---

[7] http://irisheyesgardenseeds.com
[8] http://www.denverpost.com/grow/ci_14839542
[9] http://seattletimes.nwsource.com/html/living/2008829994_seedside09.html

the lower wood slats and digging them out, while those on top will continue growing until all potatoes are mature. This design has the potential for a truly enormous harvest.

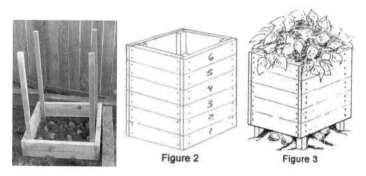

Figure 2   **Figure 3**

The Seattle Times followed a gardener's attempt to construct the box and grow some potatoes, which yielded only 25 pounds rather than 100. A yield of 25 pounds still is far more than you could ever grow in the same amount of space using traditional methods. But apparently, the yield was that low because they grew the wrong variety. Only vigorous, late-maturing potatoes will produce more heavily using this method. Mr. Lutovsky recommends only using Yellow Finn, Indian Pit, Red Pontiac, or fingerling types.

If that plan is too difficult, you can try another one that I prefer. I did not invent it, and there are as many examples of this idea all over the Internet as there are references to the Lutovsky box. I am merely passing the concept along to you and telling you that it works, because I have used it successfully myself.

The plan is this: Grow your spuds in a garbage can. Find a nice tall one and wash it out really, really well. I mean that, since you'll be growing a food crop. Better yet, buy a brand new container for this.

I bought a 32 gallon Rubbermaid brand plastic garbage can for $18 at a hardware store. I washed it out and drilled about 20 evenly spaced holes in the sides and a few more in the bottom. I then put a few shovelfuls of loose, composty soil at the bottom to a height of about six inches, placed several pieces of seed potatoes inside, and covered these with 3-4 more inches of soil which I sprinkled with organic fertilizer. As the potatoes grew, I covered part of the emerging stem each time (Mr. Lutovsky says to cover only ¼ of the stem each time, but I just don't get out to the garden often enough to do that much regular hilling). I picked 42 pounds of taters from my garbage bucket, and I must have forgotten to water it for at least a couple of weeks during the worst of the summer, which no doubt cost me some additional spuds.

Another approach, which other gardeners have reported works well, is to cut out the bottom of the plastic garbage can and plant your seed potatoes in the ground soil, surrounding them with the rest of the garbage can (which might need some stakes to hold it in place). In all honesty, I would recommend this method above mine, as it gives you even more growing height, provided that you plant the potatoes (and garbage can) on some nice, loose, fertile soil. The only reason I don't do it this way is that I have gophers below. I have not tried it yet on top of a raised bed, but that should work quite nicely.

Whether you plant the seed potatoes in the ground or near the bottom of a vertical container, this method should yield a very large harvest. But do not forget you also need to fertilize the plants and keep them well watered throughout the growing season. You could experiment with a fertilizer that is slightly higher than usual in nitrogen, since this involves a great deal of stem growth. I would look for something with an N-P-K number starting with 7 or so, or else supplement with some feather meal, cottonseed meal, or liquid fish fertilizer (I know, it sounds yucky, but it really works).

Speaking of a maritime ingredient that really works, check out this next Secret Tip for a way to boost your potato plants' growth rate and put you on your way to a harvest of the most delicious tasting spuds you've ever had.

Secret Tip #2: Nourish Your Plants with a Special Treat

Plants love to be pampered. It is one thing to give them their minimum nutritional requirements via fertilizer. You can live on food rations, too. But if you give them some special treats just like a child or a pet, they will show you some real love!

Tomatoes are America's favorite homegrown crop, and with good reason. But potatoes have become very popular for home growing as well due to the energy and food value they deliver. Once you have tasted your own homegrown potatoes from varieties you will never find in the stores, you'll be hooked on growing them at home also.

Both potatoes and tomatoes are from the same family and have similar nutritional needs. Basically, both of them are very simple plants to grow at home. But if you want the tastiest and most productive tomatoes and potatoes, you must be prepared to take one or two additional steps. With the huge popularity and all the expert research that exists on growing tomatoes, it took me a whole booklet to explain just five tips for growing bigger and better tomatoes. For potatoes, I am condensing it a bit. If there is just *one* extra step you should take to ensure more productive and tastier spuds, this is it: spray the plants' leaves with diluted kelp extract.

Kelp, *Ascophyllum nodosum*, is a huge seaweed that grows near the coast in cool ocean waters. Perhaps you have seen massive strands of kelp wash up on a beach or you have visited an aquarium with a breathtaking kelp forest exhibit like the one in the picture below. The exhibit at the Monterey Bay Aquarium in California has kelp strands that reach three stories high, while the picture below shows a tank at Two Oceans Aquarium in Capetown, South Africa. Kelp is one of the fastest growing plants in the world, able to grow as much as *four feet* in a single day under the right conditions.

Not surprisingly, the plant contains very high levels of natural growth stimulants. While you can harvest kelp at the beach for your use in the garden, it is not as potent as the concentrated forms you can buy. Kelp also provides a good source of potassium (potash) and trace minerals for potatoes, which they very much need and may not get from your soil or fertilizer. Giving your plants a kelp treat will improve both potato productivity and flavor.

Several kelp products are available at nurseries and online stores for use in the home garden. Liquid kelp extract can be diluted and sprayed on your plants' leaves as a foliar fertilizer. The plants are able to take up nutrients that are dissolved in water and applied to their leaves. Kelp meal powder can be added to your soil directly or mixed in water if it is soluble. I use the liquid extract, following the label directions on the back to dilute it in water. Then I spray it on the plant leaves at least once a month. I use either a large garden sprayer (like the kind used for spraying chemicals) or a small hand spray bottle. Both are available at nurseries. Alternatively, you can just dump some kelpy water at the base of the plant, which is called a soil drench.

Some believe that kelp extract makes a plant much healthier and less susceptible to disease. I don't know whether that's true, but it would not surprise me. I just know that regularly spraying your tomato plants with this stuff is the next best thing to feeding them sugar cubes (just kidding). And for potatoes, it seems to really increase plant growth and result in more tubers. There is no scientific evidence that these spuds are better tasting, but I have my opinion. Try this tip, then taste some potatoes for yourself. Let me know what you think!

Author Info

R.J. Ruppenthal is a licensed attorney and college professor who has a passion for growing and raising some of his own food. He is based in California, though he has experience trying to grow winter vegetables in Wisconsin. He regularly writes and blogs about fruit and vegetable gardening, growing food in small urban spaces, sustainability, and raising backyard chickens. On occasion, he even pens something about law or government. You can follow his blogs at http://www.amazon.com/R.J.-Ruppenthal/e/B00852ZTT2/ref=ntt_athr_dp_pel_1

My Publications

1. *Fall and Winter Gardening: 25 Organic Vegetables to Plant and Grow for Late Season Food*

Description from Amazon:
Complete guide to growing organic vegetables for a fall and winter garden. This book explains which vegetables can survive in cold weather and how to grow them. Recommended for backyard gardeners and container gardeners who want to grow food for fresh eating all year round.

Topics Include

- Introduction to Late Season Vegetable Gardening
- 25 Vegetables for Cool Seasons
- Starting Vegetables From Seed
- When to Plant in Your Area
- Preparing the Soil and Fertilizing
- Garden Rows, Raised Beds, and Containers
- Extending Your Season
- Harvesting and Storing Your Produce
- Resources: More Information

2. *Backyard Chickens for Beginners: Getting the Best Chickens, Choosing Coops, Feeding and Care, and Beating City Chicken Laws*

Description from Amazon:
Excellent booklet for beginners on how to start a backyard mini-flock of 2-4 chickens and get fresh eggs every day. Written by the author of the best-selling Fresh Food From Small Spaces book, a former columnist for Urban Farm magazine. (Updated 2012 Version)

Topics include:
• Fresh Eggs Every Day

- How Much Space Do You Need?
- Building or Buying a Coop
- Feeders, Waterers, Nesting Boxes, and Roosts
- Getting Chicks or Chickens
- Feeding Your Chickens
- Tips for Cold Climates
- Health and Safety
- Dealing with Neighbors, City Chicken Laws, and Other Challenges
- Resources: Everything You Need!

3. *How to Sprout Raw Food: Grow an Indoor Organic Garden with Wheatgrass, Bean Sprouts, Grain Sprouts, Microgreens, and More*

Description from Amazon:

Grow Your Own Raw Food Anywhere!
Would you like to grow some of your own food this year? Indoors? With no sunlight or soil? At any time of the year and at all times of the year? Sprouts allow you to do all that and more. In fact, you can grow all the vegetables your body needs (plus all the protein as well) in an area that's no bigger than your microwave oven. I grow sprouts on top of my refrigerator, harvesting baskets of fresh, raw food every week without even going outside.

Growing sprouts is simple and it's cheap. Sprouts can provide you with the power-packed nutrition your body needs at a fraction of the price of store bought food. You can save money while eating right. There's no dirt, no pests, and no weeding required.

Raw Food Salads, Sandwiches, Cereals, and More!
This short guide will teach you how to grow sprouts and enjoy eating them. If you like salads, I'll show you how to make delicious bowlfuls with tasty mild or spicy sprouts. If you enjoy eating cereal for breakfast, try some sprouted grains with natural malt sugars that nourish your body and taste far better than boxed cereals.

Need to lose a few pounds?
Simply eating a few more sprouted beans will keep you feeling fuller and eating fewer carbs. Toss some bean sprouts, lentil sprouts, or pea sprouts into your next rice or pasta dish; they make great burgers as well. You'll find that your body absorbs the protein better when the beans are

sprouted, which usually reduces flatulence as well. All this nutrition, protein, and fiber will have you shedding a few pounds in a hurry.

Topics Include:

1. Superfood Sprouts
Cheap, Easy to Grow, Provide Year-Round Nutrition

2. The Benefits of Raw Food
Lose Weight, Nourish Your Body, and Stimulate Energy Levels

3. Sprouting Equipment and How to Use It
Trays, Jars, Bags, Automatic Sprouters, and Wheatgrass Juicers

4. Salad and Sandwich Sprouts
Alfalfa, Clover, Radish, and Broccoli

5. Bean Sprouts
Mung Beans, Soy Beans, Lentils, Peas, and More

6. Grain Sprouts
Wheat, Barley, Rye, Oats, Triticale, Quinoa, and Other Grains

7. Seed and Nut Sprouts
Sunflower, Sesame, Pumpkin, Peanut, and Flax

8. Seasoning Sprouts
Basil, Celery, Cress, Dill, Fenugreek, Mustard, Onion Family, and More

9. How to Grow Microgreens
Grow a Gourmet Baby Salad, Anytime, Anyplace!

10. Wheatgrass Juice From Homegrown Sprouts
How to Grow and Juice Your Own Wheatgrass

11. Where to Get the Best Sprouting Seeds
Trusted Sources for the Freshest Quality

12. Where to Find the Best Raw Food Sprout Recipes
Delicious ways to enjoy your sprouts, raw or cooked

4. *Blueberries in Your Backyard: How to Grow America's Hottest Antioxidant Fruit for Food, Health, and Extra Money*

Description from Amazon:

Perfect blueberry growing guide for beginners. This booklet explains how to plant and grow blueberries in the home garden. Recommended for backyard gardeners with small city-sized yards, patios, balconies, decks, and rooftops. (Updated 2012 version)

Topics include:

- Why Grow Blueberries? Six Great Reasons
- Blueberries for Every Climate (and where to get them)
- Grow Blueberries Almost Anywhere: Doorsteps, Patios, Balconies, Rooftops, and Yards
- Perfect Blueberry Soil (regular garden soil kills them, but they will thrive in this!)
- How to Plant and Grow Blueberries in Raised Beds and Containers
- Feeding, Watering, and Caring for Your Blueberry Bushes
- Making Extra Money Growing Blueberries

Photo credits: Cover: Fotosearch, copyright "Trudy", www.fotosearch.com
and CanStockPhoto, www.canstockphoto.com
Raised bed on lawn: Flickr user "Truk", www.flickr.com
Kelp forest: Flick user "Coda", www.flickr.com
Other photos: Rights held by author or public domain

20211858R00016

Made in the USA
Lexington, KY
24 January 2013